W9-BFB-111

Book Design: MaryJane Wojciechowski
Contributing Editors: Jennifer Ceaser and Rob Kirkpatrick

Photo Credits: pp. 4-5 © Bettmann/Corbis; p 7 © Dave Bartruff/Corbis; pp. 8-9 © Dave Stock/All Sport; p. 11 © Jim Sugar Photography/Corbis; p. 12 © Marvin J. Fryer/National Geographic; p. 14 © Dewitt Jones/Corbis; p. 17 © Susan Sanford/National Geographic; p. 18 © Reuters/Thomas Szlukovenyi/Archive Photos; pp. 20-21 © AFP/Corbis; p. 22 © Vince Streano/Corbis; p. 25 © James Blair/National Geographic; p. 29 © Winfield Parks/National Geographic; pp. 30-31 © Michael Maslan Historic Photographs/Corbis; pp. 33, 34 © Roger Ressmeyer/Corbis; p. 38 © Reuters/Toshiyuki Aizawa/Archive Photos

Visit Children's Press on the Internet at:
http://publishing.grolier.com

Library of Congress Cataloging-in-Publication Data

Thompson, Luke.
    Earthquakes / by Luke Thompson.
      p. cm.—(Natural disasters)
    Includes index.
    Summary: Explains why earthquakes occur and describes the technology used to study them, the damage they inflict, and some of the more famous earthquakes in history.
    ISBN 0-516-23366-1 (lib. bdg.)—ISBN 0-516-23566-4 (pbk.)
      1. Earthquakes—Juvenile literature. [1. Earthquakes.] I. Title. II. Natural disasters
    (Children's Press)

QE521.3 .T53 2000
551.22—dc21
                                                            99-058297

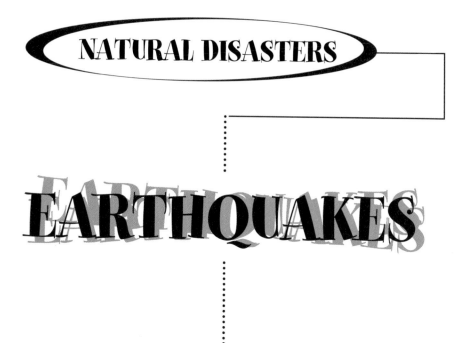

NATURAL DISASTERS

EARTHQUAKES

Luke Thompson

HIGH
interest
books

Children's Press
A Division of Grolier Publishing
New York / London / Hong Kong / Sydney
Danbury, Connecticut

CONTENTS

INTRODUCTION

On November 1, 1755, the city of Lisbon, Portugal was preparing for an important religious holiday. Most of the city's 250,000 residents were attending church.

Without warning, a huge earthquake rocked the city. Churches, buildings, and houses all over the city crumbled. Streets cracked open and caved in. Roofs fell, crushing people below. There was so much dust that the sun was blocked out. The sky over Lisbon turned dark.

One resident described the disaster: "The earthquake shook my house with such violence that the upper stories immediately fell. I expected to be crushed to death, as the walls rocked to and fro in the most frightful manner. Large stones fell down on every side of me. The sky in a moment became so gloomy that I could not see."

Lisbon, Portugal, after the 1755 earthquake

EARTHQUAKES

Citizens rushed to the shore to escape the collapsing city. Moments later, giant ocean waves surged toward the beaches. The 20-foot (6-m) waves crashed on the shore, drowning thousands of helpless people.

The Lisbon earthquake lasted for ten minutes. It left more than sixty thousand people dead—almost one quarter of the city's population. It was one of the largest-known earthquakes in human history, covering 1.5 million square miles (3.9 million sq. km). The effects of the quake could be felt as far away as Africa and America. At that time, many people thought it was a sign of the end of the world.

An earthquake is one of the Earth's most violent and deadly natural disasters. During an earthquake, the ground trembles and shakes. The earth cracks open. Buildings collapse, bridges crumble, and streets break apart. People are hurt or killed by falling wreckage.

Memorial to the people who died in the 1755 Lisbon earthquake

Introduction

Often other natural disasters, such as avalanches, follow an earthquake. Tsunamis (huge ocean waves) can cause damage along the coast. Fires result from broken gas and power lines. Cities are flooded as water pipes crack from the force of the quake.

Worldwide, there are about eighteen powerful earthquakes each year. These earthquakes are responsible for billions of dollars' worth of damage and the loss of tens of thousands of lives.

CHAPTER ONE

WHEN THE EARTH MOVES

On the evening of October 17, 1989, the third game of the World Series between the San Francisco Giants and the Oakland Athletics was about to begin. Then, just before the baseball game started, a massive earthquake hit the San Francisco area. The stadium started shaking. Terrified fans rushed out of the stadium. Fortunately, no one in the stadium was injured. But the rest of San Francisco was not so lucky.

Across the city, buildings collapsed. Some buildings sank straight into the ground. A large section of the San Francisco-Oakland Bay Bridge crashed into the water. Some people were driving across the bridge when the earthquake hit. One driver remembered: "I slammed on the brakes and stopped just before the broken edge. If I'd gone any farther, I would have fallen to my death in the water

1989 World Series at San Francisco's Candlestick Park

below." People caught on the bridge had to be saved by rescue teams.

The earthquake lasted only fifteen seconds, but it caused a lot of damage. Enormous sections of California's freeways fell apart. Overpasses crumbled. Falling concrete and steel crushed cars and trucks. About thirty separate fires broke out in the city. Electric power was knocked out for three days.

In the end, sixty-two people in California lost their lives. More than twelve thousand people lost their homes. The earthquake caused more than six billion dollars' worth of damage.

For centuries, human beings have tried to figure out why earthquakes happen. We take for granted that we have solid ground underneath us. When that solid ground suddenly begins shaking and breaking apart, we want to know why. We also want to know if and when it will happen again.

The 1989 earthquake caused huge sections of San Francisco's Cypress freeway to fall apart.

WHERE QUAKES FIND THEIR START

Earth is made up of three layers of rock: core, mantle, and crust. The center of Earth is called the core. The core is made of solid rock surrounded by a layer of hot, liquid rock. The middle section is called the mantle. The mantle is made mostly of solid rock with small areas of liquid rock. The topmost layer is called the crust. Made of solid rock, the crust covers the surface of Earth like a shell.

Tectonic plates slide against each other and can become stuck.

Earth's crust is broken into nine larger—
and at least twelve smaller—slabs of rock.
These slabs, which can be up to 62 miles (100
km) thick, are called tectonic plates. Tectonic
plates are constantly moving—either pulling
away from or pushing against one another.
The plates move very slowly, so you cannot
actually feel the ground moving. But as tectonic plates move, they scrape against each
other. Some plates run into each other head-on.

When the Earth Moves

Some plates slide past each other and then become stuck. Plates also can rub against each other for long periods of time. Earthquakes begin in Earth's crust where these plates meet.

Faults

The place where tectonic plates meet is called a fault. Faults are fractures, or cracks, in Earth's crust. Faults are a result of tectonic plates colliding over millions of years. The plates are put under so much strain that, eventually, they crack. Large blocks of rock then shift past each other along the crack. The rock on one side of the crack will shift up, down, or sideways as the rock on the other side shifts in the opposite direction. This rock movement creates an area with a lot of faults. An area with many faults is called a fault zone.

Faults can range in size from inches to thousands of miles in length. The bigger the fault, the greater the chance that an earthquake will

occur there. A large fault also may signal that the size of the earthquake will be large, too.

WHAT CAUSES A QUAKE?

Over time, as tectonic plates grind against each other, pressure begins to build. As the plates push against each other, they begin to crack. The stress on the plates becomes so great that the Earth needs a way to release the pressure. This release comes in the form of a sudden burst of energy. Usually the stored-up energy will be released at the

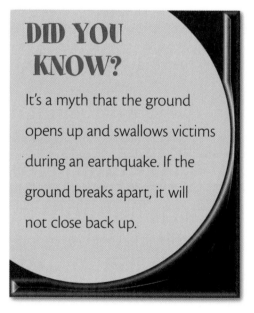

DID YOU KNOW?

It's a myth that the ground opens up and swallows victims during an earthquake. If the ground breaks apart, it will not close back up.

weakest point of the Earth's crust. The weakest point is on a fault, where there is already a

The San Andreas Fault runs for about 600 miles (966 km) through California.

crack in the crust. The burst of energy causes a section of the fault to break loose. Then the two halves of the fault bounce past each other. This rock movement creates the strong shaking of an earthquake.

Shock Waves

The burst of energy that is released by the fault comes in waves of motion. These waves are called seismic waves, or shock waves. Shock waves occur when the pressure between tectonic plates is released. Shock waves cause the earth to vibrate (shake) violently, which is what we feel on the Earth's surface as an earthquake.

Shock waves are invisible. If you could see them, they would look like waves in an ocean. You may not be able to see shock waves, but you certainly can feel them. The shock waves of large earthquakes are very powerful. They start from the center of the

Shock waves travel outward in circles from an earthquake's epicenter.

earthquake, which is called the epicenter. Shock waves travel upward and outward from the epicenter in a circular motion. They travel through the ground extremely fast. Shock waves can cover a distance of a hundred miles in a matter of a few seconds. Sometimes the waves can be felt hundreds of miles from the earthquake's epicenter.

A collapsed hotel after the September 1999 earthquake in Taiwan

FORESHOCKS, MAINSHOCKS, AND AFTERSHOCKS

Earthquakes come in groups. An earthquake may begin with foreshocks. Foreshocks are small tremors (vibrations) that are created when faults begin to release pressure. Foreshocks indicate that a larger mainshock will hit. The mainshock is the actual main earthquake. The mainshock is the strongest of the quakes.

After a major or even a moderate main-shock, smaller earthquakes usually occur. These smaller quakes are called aftershocks. Aftershocks happen when an earthquake does not relieve all of the pressure that has built up in the rocks of the Earth's crust.

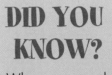

DID YOU KNOW?

When you see the damage that major earthquakes cause, you may think that the tremors of an earthquake last a long time. In fact, earthquake tremors usually last for only ten to fifteen seconds.

As the rocks settle down, several after-shocks can occur in the hours following a quake. Aftershocks may last for days, weeks, and sometimes even months after an earthquake. Even the largest aftershock will not be as violent as the mainshock. However, aftershocks still can cause a lot of damage. Structures weakened from the mainshock can easily collapse when an aftershock hits.

TIPPING THE SCALES

Izmit is a Turkish city that lies on the North Anatolian Fault. The North Anatolian Fault is a 500-mile (805-km) fault that runs across Turkey. On August 17, 1999, this fault suddenly gave way.

Within seconds, Izmit began to crumble. One shocked citizen recalled, "When the house started to shake, I ran outside to the balcony. I thought, 'This is it. This is my last moment on Earth.'"

Another resident remembered the terrifying moments as her apartment building collapsed: "The ground opened up and there was a huge crash. Suddenly I wasn't on the third floor anymore. The street was right outside my window."

Thousands of Turkish citizens were crushed under the roofs and walls of falling buildings. Many were trapped in collapsed buildings

Searching for survivors after the deadly 1999 earthquake in Izmit, Turkey

A seismologist checks readings on a seismograph

where they suffocated (ran out of air) and died. More than twenty thousand people died in the earthquake in Turkey. Another fifty thousand people were injured. It was one of the worst disasters of the century.

Some earthquakes, such as the one described above, are very powerful. They break up the Earth with the strength of thousands of bombs. People can feel the ground shaking, even if they are hundreds of miles from the center of the quake. These quakes cause millions of dollars of property damage and kill people by the thousands.

Other earthquakes, though, take place without harming anyone. These quakes are so small that no one can feel them. Even some large earthquakes can be harmless if they strike in an area where no people live.

SEIS-ING UP AN EARTHQUAKE

Scientists who study earthquakes are called seismologists. Seismologists spend their time studying the vibrations that happen in the Earth. One instrument used by seismologists is called a seismograph. A seismograph determines the time and the place that an earthquake occurs. It also measures the quake's strength. A seismograph can figure out this data by recording the motion of the ground during an earthquake.

EARTHQUAKES

A seismograph has a frame with a needle and a long sheet of paper attached. As the ground shakes, the needle draws lines on the paper to show the vibrations. These vibrations are the seismic waves that occur during an earthquake. The seismograph records these vibrations over a specific period of time. When the needle makes a long line, that means that the movement is very strong. The more powerful the quake, the longer the lines and the closer together they are.

Seismologists then compare this data with the data from past earthquakes. This comparison allows seismologists to track how many earthquakes occur around a particular fault. They can use the information to analyze how much activity there is around the fault. The scientists also use seismographs to measure the strength of foreshocks. This data can help seismologists to predict when another, larger quake might occur.

Charles Richter, cofounder of the Richter scale

MAGNITUDE

Another job of seismologists is to determine the magnitude of an earthquake. Magnitude is the measure of how big an earthquake is, or how much it shakes the earth. Seismologists use a system called the Richter scale to measure magnitude. Scientists Charles F. Richter and Beno Gutenberg invented the Richter scale in 1935.

The Richter scale places an earthquake's magnitude on a scale of 1 to 10. Most earthquakes measure less than a 2.5 on the Richter scale. These earthquakes are too small to do any serious damage. There might be a hundred of these earthquakes around the world in a single hour. We do not even feel these small quakes. Usually, a quake must be in the moderate range before we can feel it.

On the Richter scale, a one-point change indicates that a quake is ten times as strong. So, with every one-point change, the magnitude is multiplied by ten. In other words, a quake with a magnitude of 7 has one hundred times the shaking motion of a magnitude 5 quake.

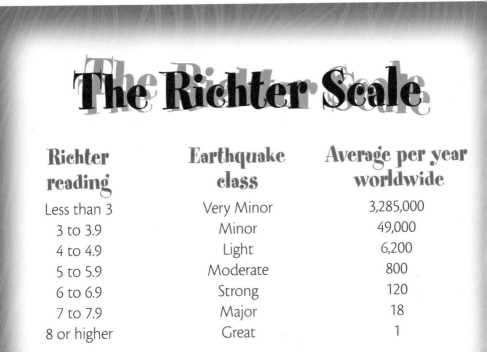

The Richter Scale

Richter reading	Earthquake class	Average per year worldwide
Less than 3	Very Minor	3,285,000
3 to 3.9	Minor	49,000
4 to 4.9	Light	6,200
5 to 5.9	Moderate	800
6 to 6.9	Strong	120
7 to 7.9	Major	18
8 or higher	Great	1

The largest earthquake ever officially recorded was an 8.9 in Japan in 1933. The strongest earthquake in the United States was an 8.5 in Anchorage, Alaska, in 1964. Scientists believe that the 1755 Lisbon earthquake would have measured an 8.75 or greater on the Richter scale.

The Richter scale is useful for measuring the force of an earthquake. However, it does not always reflect the damage done by a quake. For example, if a major earthquake (7–7.9) hit a desert that had no people or buildings, it would not cause a lot of damage. However, a moderate earthquake (5–5.9) might do a lot of damage if it hit a

DID YOU KNOW?

Earthquakes also occur on the moon. They are called moon-quakes. Most moonquakes have a magnitude of less than 2.

large city. To measure the amount of damage done by an earthquake, scientists use the Mercalli scale.

MERCALLI SCALE

The Mercalli scale was invented in 1931 by American seismologists Frank Neumann and Harry Wood. It was created to measure the effects of an earthquake on people and structures. The scale measures an earthquake on a scale of 1 to 12, using Roman numerals (I–XII). The higher the number on the scale, the more destructive the earthquake.

For example, on the Mercalli scale, a number III (3) means that the quake can be felt by people only if they are indoors. Hanging objects may swing. The vibration would be the same as the one from a large truck driving past. Most people won't recognize it as a quake. However, a number IX (9) means that people generally have started to panic. There

The Anchorage, Alaska, earthquake of 1964

is a lot of damage to buildings, and a number of structures have collapsed. Buildings have shifted off their foundations and underground pipes have broken. Cracks in the earth become apparent.

CHAPTER THREE

PREDICTION AND SAFETY

On April 18, 1906, at 5:12 in the morning, citizens along the California coast were sleeping peacefully. Several miles offshore, seismic waves moved along the San Andreas Fault. These waves traveled at a speed of 2 miles (3.2 km) per second, ripping open the ocean floor. When this earthquake struck land, it was moving at 7,000 miles (11,270 km) per hour. Several towns north of San Francisco were destroyed. Old cliffs fell into the water and new cliffs rose out of the ground.

At 5:13 A.M., the streets of San Francisco began cracking apart. Buildings shook and crumbled. Several hundred people died in their sleep as falling roofs crushed them.

The earthquake lasted forty seconds. After the shaking stopped, fires spread throughout the city. More than two thousand people died in these fires. A quarter of a million people

What was left of San Francisco's city hall after the 1906 earthquake

watched their homes burn to the ground. It was one of America's worst natural disasters.

In 1906, scientists did not have the technology that they have today to learn about earthquakes. Modern tools used by today's seismologists are far more effective. Seismologists can't yet say exactly when and where a quake will occur. However, new technology is improving their predictions. Seismologists now have hi-tech meters that are buried deep underground in faults. The meters measure the activity near a particular fault. They also monitor how much pressure is building around a fault.

Seismologists are experimenting with lasers and global positioning satellite systems to develop models of faults. These tools help scientists to study plate movement in the Earth's crust. The more seismologists know about plate movement, the better they can predict when and where a quake may happen. Today's

Today's scientists use lasers to study earthquakes.

scientists use plate tectonics (the study of plate movement) to predict where 90 percent of Earth's major earthquakes are likely to occur.

Scientists also study the number of earthquakes that have happened in an area. They use this information to predict if and when another quake will occur. For example, there were four major earthquakes in the San Francisco Bay area between 1979 and 1989.

A scientist using satellite technology to measure a fault

Seismologists believe all of this quake activity means that the San Andreas Fault is becoming more and more unstable. Scientists predict that there is a 67 percent chance that a major earthquake (magnitude 7 or larger) will strike the area in the next thirty years.

QUAKE FORECASTING

Today's scientists are sure enough about their predictions to issue earthquake warnings.

These warnings alert local governments and residents to prepare for a large earthquake. Warnings also give search-and-rescue teams time to organize.

Earthquake warnings are not as accurate as those issued for other natural disasters, such as hurricanes. Earthquake forecasting is still a new science. Earthquake forecasts are based on probability. This means that scientists can state that an earthquake probably will strike within a certain period of time.

For example, in June 1988, a magnitude 5.1 quake hit an area just outside San Francisco. Based on studies done in the area, scientists determined that a larger quake would soon strike. They stated that there was a one-in-twenty chance that a bigger quake would occur in the next five days. Earthquake warnings were issued to the public. However, nothing happened. One year later, another small quake struck the same area. Once again, a similar earthquake warning was issued. Again, the warning period went by with no earthquake activity. But sixty-nine days later, the area was struck by a magnitude 7.1 quake, known as the Loma Prieta earthquake. Sixty-three people died. The region suffered six billion dollars in damage.

Scientists were not able to determine the exact day of the Loma Prieta quake. In fact, they were about two months off. However, local governments still found the warnings helpful. They practiced what the different city departments would do in the event of a quake. So when the quake actually did strike, emergency teams were prepared to respond.

DAMAGE CONTROL

Scientists try to predict not only when an earthquake will occur, but also how much damage it will cause. They study the types of structures near faults. Many deaths caused by earthquakes are because of badly constructed buildings. Scientists help architects design buildings that will be strong enough to hold up during a quake.

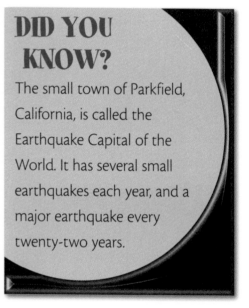

DID YOU KNOW?

The small town of Parkfield, California, is called the Earthquake Capital of the World. It has several small earthquakes each year, and a major earthquake every twenty-two years.

Architects use materials that can bend, such as steel, to construct buildings and bridges. These materials can bend or sway when the ground shakes. Those structures made from materials that are not flexible, such as bricks, quickly can fall apart from the shock of an earthquake.

HOW TO SURVIVE AN EARTHQUAKE

An earthquake can be a frightening event. Many people start to panic when everything

During a quake, you should get under a desk or table and hang onto it.

around them suddenly begins shaking. An earthquake strikes so quickly that people may not be aware of what is happening. It is necessary to know what to do during a quake.

Earthquake Dos and Don'ts

• If you are indoors, stay there! Get under a desk or table and hang onto it.

• Stay away from windows, fireplaces, heavy furniture, and appliances. Stay out of the kitchen where there are sharp objects.

• Don't stand in a door frame. Most door frames are not stronger than any other part of a house. Also, the door may swing and injure you.

• Don't run outside during an earthquake. Many people are killed just outside of buildings as bricks and other debris fall on them.

• If you are outside, get into the open. Stay away from buildings, bridges, power lines, chimneys, and anything else that might fall on you.

• Stay out of elevators. Don't use stairways unless you have to.

• If you are in a car, don't stop on or under a bridge or freeway overpass.

Fact Sheet ·········

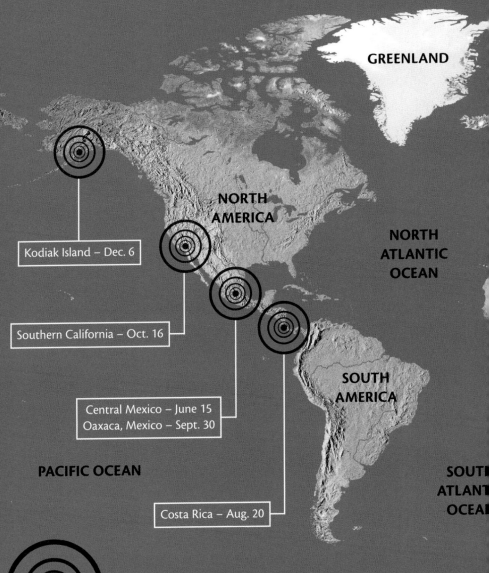

GREENLAND

NORTH
AMERICA

NORTH
ATLANTIC
OCEAN

Kodiak Island – Dec. 6

Southern California – Oct. 16

Central Mexico – June 15
Oaxaca, Mexico – Sept. 30

SOUTH
AMERICA

PACIFIC OCEAN

SOUT
ATLANT
OCEA

Costa Rica – Aug. 20

The circles on the map show where earthquakes with a
magnitude of 7–7.9 occurred in 1999.

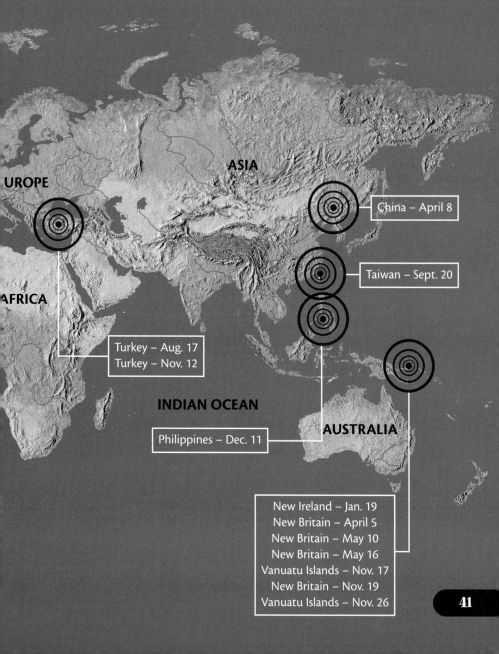

1999 Earthquakes

ASIA

UROPE

China – April 8

Taiwan – Sept. 20

AFRICA

Turkey – Aug. 17
Turkey – Nov. 12

INDIAN OCEAN

AUSTRALIA

Philippines – Dec. 11

New Ireland – Jan. 19
New Britain – April 5
New Britain – May 10
New Britain – May 16
Vanuatu Islands – Nov. 17
New Britain – Nov. 19
Vanuatu Islands – Nov. 26

41

NEW WORDS

aftershock a smaller earthquake that happens after the main earthquake

architect a person who designs structures

core the center of Earth, made of solid rock and surrounded by a layer of hot, liquid rock

crust the topmost layer of Earth

epicenter the center of an earthquake

fault a fracture or crack in the Earth's crust

fault zone an area with a lot of faults

flexible able to bend

foreshock a small tremor or vibration that is created when plates first begin to crack

global positioning satellite systems instruments that help seismologists study plate movement in the Earth's crust

magnitude size and intensity

mainshock the strongest in a series of earthquakes

mantle the middle layer of Earth, made mostly of solid rock with small areas of liquid rock

Mercalli scale the way to measure a quake's damage, based on a Roman numeral system

NEW WORDS

plate tectonics the study of tectonic plate movement

Richter scale the way of measuring the magnitude of an earthquake

seismic waves invisible shock waves that travel outward from the epicenter of an earthquake

seismograph an instrument used to record the vibrations of an earthquake

seismologist a scientist who studies earthquakes

tectonic plates slabs of rock that make up the Earth's crust

tremor shaking in the ground caused by an earthquake

tsunami an extremely large wave that can be caused by an earthquake in the ocean floor

vibrate to shake

FOR FURTHER READING

Archer, Jules. *Earthquake!* Parsippany, N.J.: Silver Burdett Press, 1991.

Field, Nancy, and Adele Schepige. *Discovering Earthquakes*. Middleton, WI.: Dog Eared Publications, 1995.

Sherrow, Victoria. *San Francisco Earthquake, 1989: Death and Destruction (American Disasters)*. Springfield, N.J.: Enslow, 1998.

Spies, Karen B. *Earthquakes (When Disaster Strikes)*. New York: Twenty First Century Books, 1995.

Federal Emergency Management Agency

Web site: *www.fema.gov/*

A site designed by the Federal Emergency Management Agency (FEMA). Includes maps of areas in danger of experiencing an earthquake or other natural disaster. Contains advice on what precautions you should take during a quake.

National Earthquake Information Center

Web site: *www.neic.cr.usgs.gov/*

A program sponsored by the United States Department of the Interior that provides information related to the Earth. Discusses ways to improve our quality of life and decrease our losses from natural disasters. The National Earthquake Information Center keeps a worldwide earthquake database that includes information on earthquakes and seismology.

RESOURCES

Southern California Earthquake Center
Web site: *www.scec.org*
A community of scientists and specialists who study earthquake hazards.

Tools of the Seismologist
Web site: *http://smjuhsd.sbceo.k12.ca.us/erhs/ science/activities/SAF/intro.html*
A virtual tour of the methods used by seismologists to study earthquakes.

U.S. Geological Society
807 National Center
Reston, VA 20192
888-275-8747
Web site: *www.usgs.gov/*
The official site of the United States Geological Society, which studies the Earth. Includes studies and predictions of earthquakes.

INDEX

INDEX

ABOUT THE AUTHOR

Luke Thompson was born in Delaware. He holds a degree in English literature from James Madison University. He currently lives in Vail, Colorado.